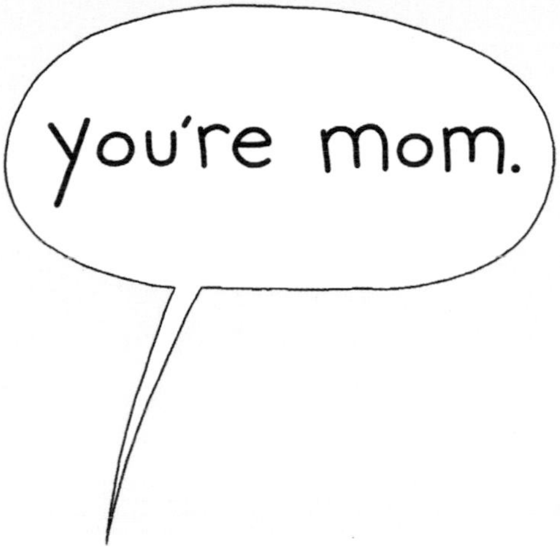
you're mom.

## ALSO BY LIZ CLIMO

*Best Bear Ever!*
*Rory the Dinosaur: Me and My Dad*
*Rory the Dinosaur Wants a Pet*
*Rory the Dinosaur Needs a Christmas Tree*
*The Little World of Liz Climo*
*Lobster is the Best Medicine*

you're mom.

# a little book for mothers

(and the people who love them)

## liz climo

FLATIRON
BOOKS
NEW YORK

YOU'RE MOM. Copyright © 2020 by Liz Climo.
All rights reserved. Printed in China.
For information, address Flatiron Books,
120 Broadway, New York, NY 10271.

www.flatironbooks.com

Designed by Steven Seighman

The Library of Congress Cataloging-in-Publication Data is available upon request.

ISBN 978-1-250-22810-9 (paper over board)
ISBN 978-1-250-22812-3 (ebook)

Our books may be purchased in bulk for promotional, educational, or business use. Please contact your local bookseller or the Macmillan Corporate and Premium Sales Department at 1-800-221-7945, extension 5442, or by email at MacmillanSpecialMarkets@macmillan.com.

First Edition: April 2020

10  9  8  7  6  5  4

*For Marlow and Mary Lou*

you're mom.

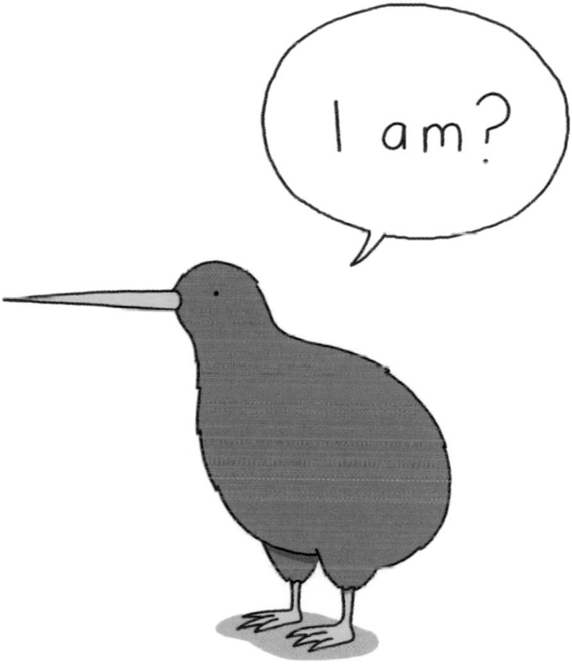
I am?

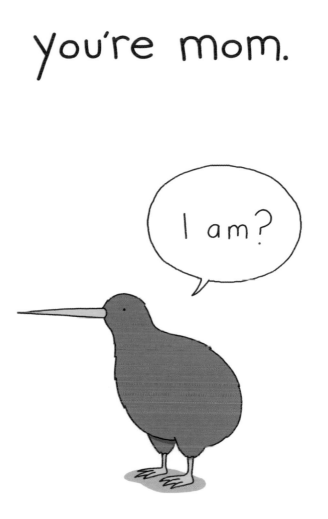

Maybe not! But you probably know a mom or a mom figure—and right now, I want to say thanks to all the moms out there. Specifically, the moms who are doing the best they can.

Full disclosure: I am a mom, but I didn't write this book about myself. (Can you imagine? *Hey everyone, aren't I the BEST? Go me!*) Yes, many of the jokes in here are based on my own experiences as a mom, but the idea for the book came from somewhere else.

Something significant happened when I became a mom (I mean, aside from not sleeping for about four months straight): It made me appreciate and feel more connected to my own mom, who died when I was twenty-two. I wrote this book for her, because she was wonderful. She wasn't perfect, of course. Like most moms, she made some mistakes and probably felt like she was doing a terrible job most of the time, but she loved her children unconditionally. She made us feel safe, and not just us—she opened her heart and door to other children who didn't feel love in their own homes. There are so many people out there like her, and if someone gave this book to you, you're probably one of them.

One of the hardest things about losing my mom at a young age was that everyone else seemed to still have their moms. That feeling of isolation lasted beyond the initial shock and heartache of losing her, and it became even more difficult after I had my own daughter. It felt so cruel that they would never get to know each other. When I was pregnant, I'd often wonder if my baby would look like her. I secretly hoped that my child's arrival would, in some way, bring my own mother back.

Then my daughter was born—with sparkly blue eyes and strawberry blond hair. She was lovely, but she didn't look a thing like my mom (or me, for that matter). She didn't really act like her, either. But that was okay! She is an entirely different person, after all.

Soon, I began to notice something: I'd catch a glimpse of my reflection in the mirror, and see my sleepy eyes and messy dark hair. I'd hear how I spoke to my daughter, or hear myself making up silly songs for her. I'd notice the way she made me laugh—a booming, unabashed laugh that I hadn't experienced in ages. And I could feel how much my daughter loved me. I recognized that feeling because I felt the same way about my own mom. Rather than seeing my mom in my daughter, I had started to see my mom in myself.

Does that mean we feel that sort of connection to our parents only when we have children of our own? Nope! That was just how I happened to get to that place—but what do I know? (Just kidding. I'm very wise. Please don't put this book down.) Some of us have children, and some of us don't. Some of us have wonderful relationships with our parents, and some of us don't. I don't want this book to be some secret handbook that only moms are allowed to have. Rather, I want to acknowledge those people out there doing the difficult and often very lonely job of being a parent, or being in a parental role. You are doing incredible things for the people who are lucky enough to be loved by you.

My own mom taught me the importance of unconditional love, acceptance, generosity, and kindness. I am grateful for all of you out there doing the same, either with your own children or just the people you surround yourself with. You make the world a much better place, and this book is for you.

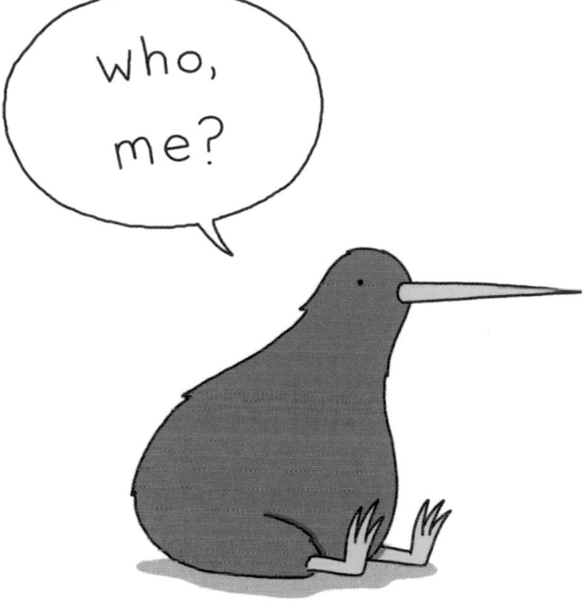
who,
me?

Yes, you. I still think you're great, by the way, whether or not you're mom.

Thanks. I hope you like it.

Liz

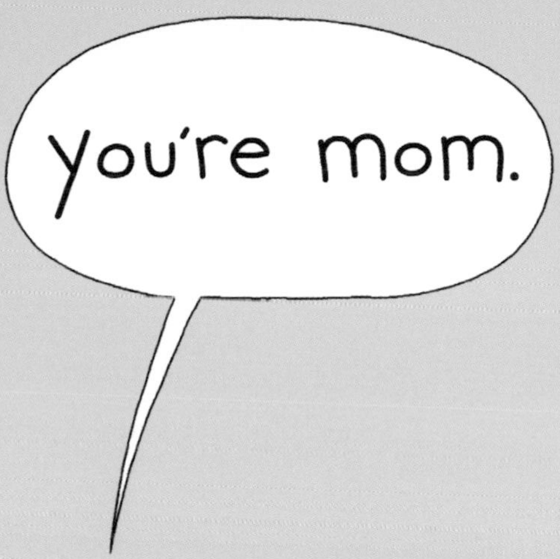
you're mom.

You're mom.

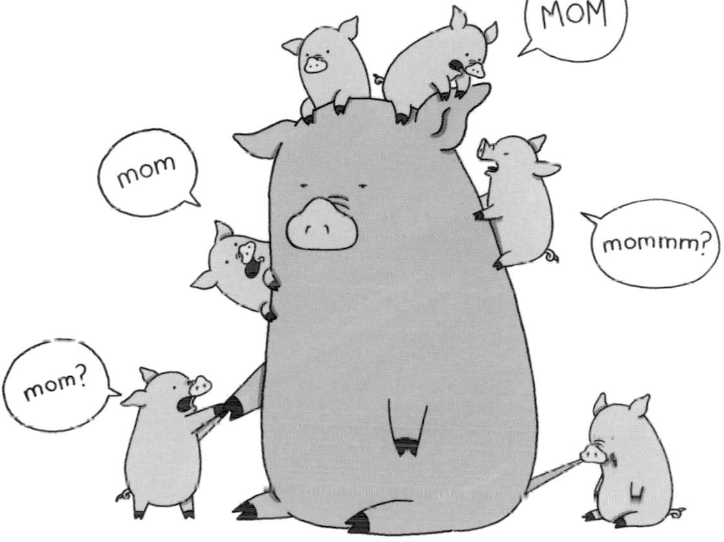
MOM
mom
mommm?
mom?

You've had to read a lot of picture books.

only this
many
more.

(And if you haven't already,
you will soon. I promise.)

So, here's a picture
book just for you.

Becoming a mom is a pretty big deal.

Sometimes, it happens fast.

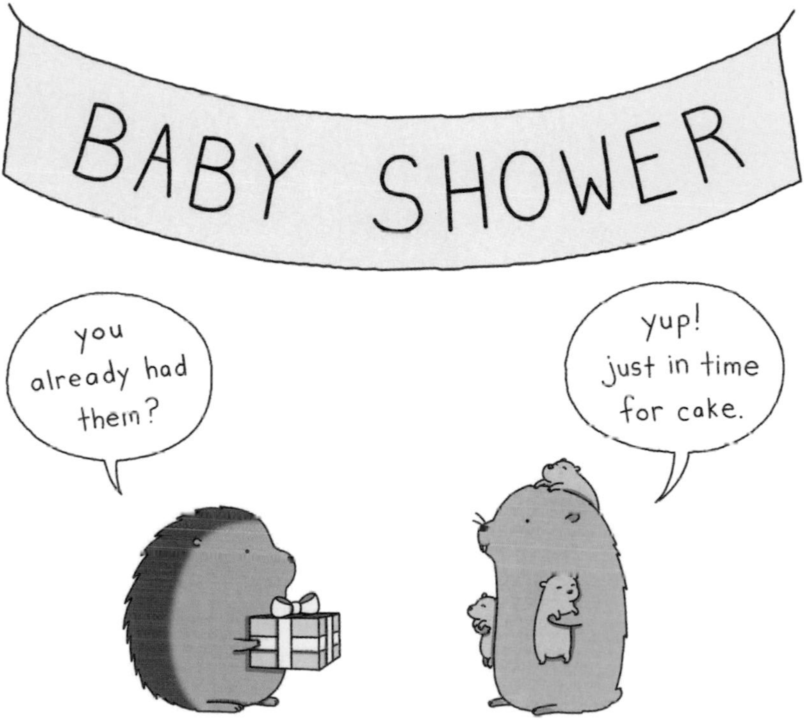
BABY SHOWER
you already had them?
yup! just in time for cake.

Sometimes, it takes a while.

geez! you're still pregnant? hasn't it been, like, two years?
don't talk to me.

Sometimes, it feels like you've been waiting forever.

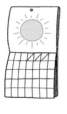

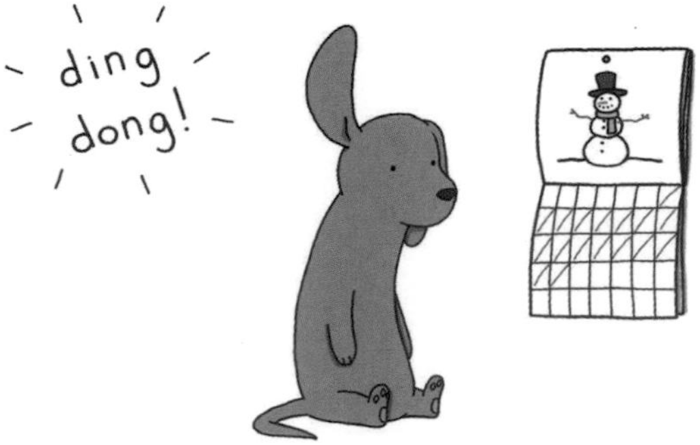
ding
dong!

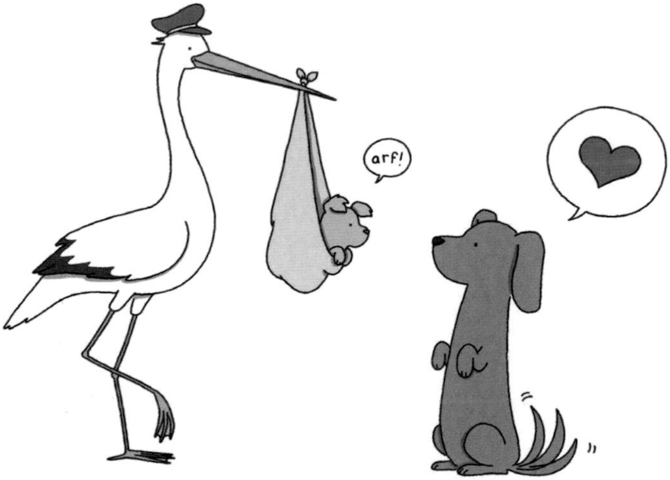
arf!

Sometimes, it's a big surprise.

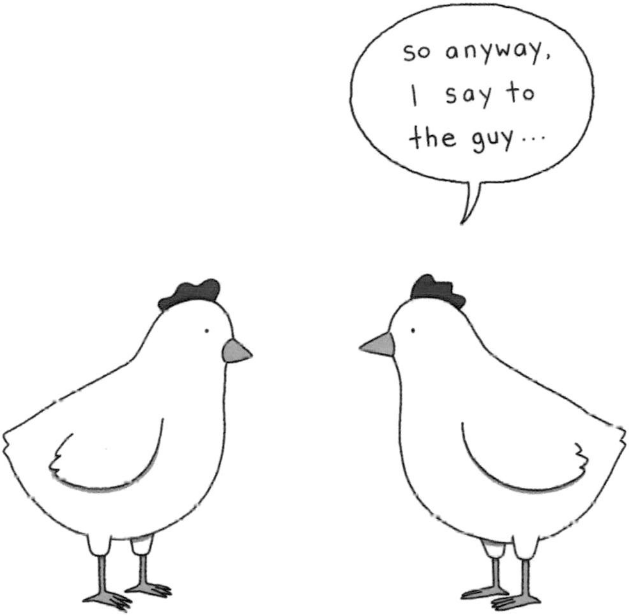
so anyway, I say to the guy...

what the...

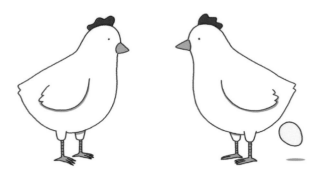

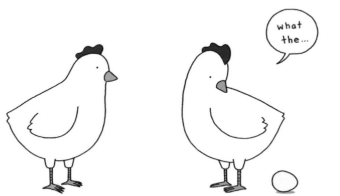

However it happens . . .

. . . this incredible journey has just begun.

Today's the day.
Your little one is finally here,

and she's perfect.

This precious gift is yours
to love forever.

How lucky are you?

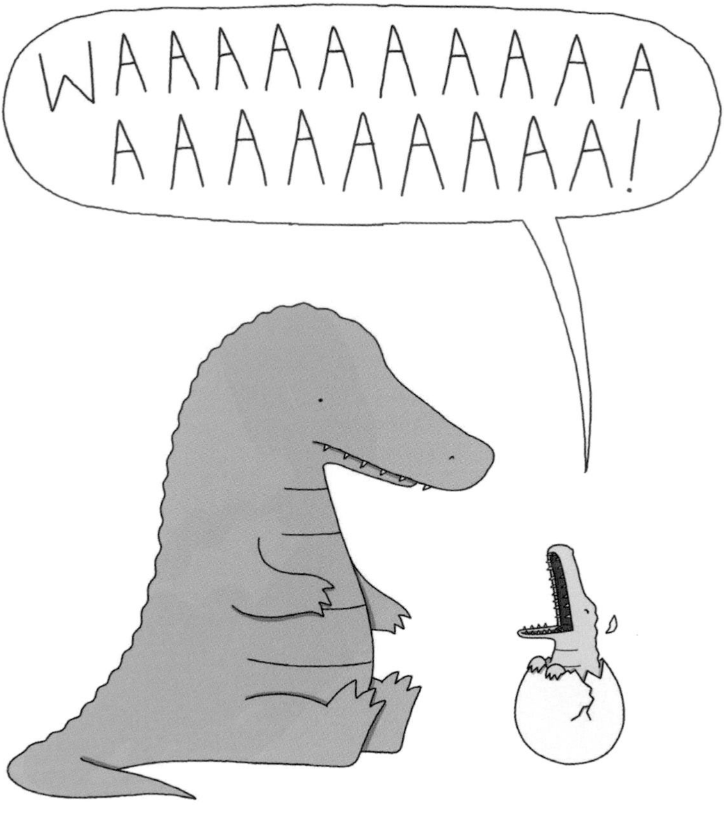
WAAAAAAAAAAAAAAAAAAA!

Sure, having a new baby can be
a little intimidating at first.

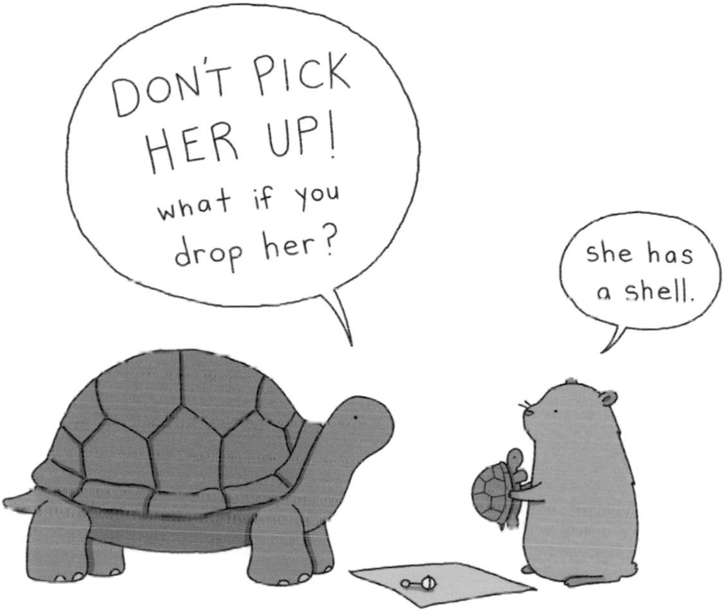
DON'T PICK HER UP! what if you drop her?
she has a shell.

Okay . . . a lot intimidating.

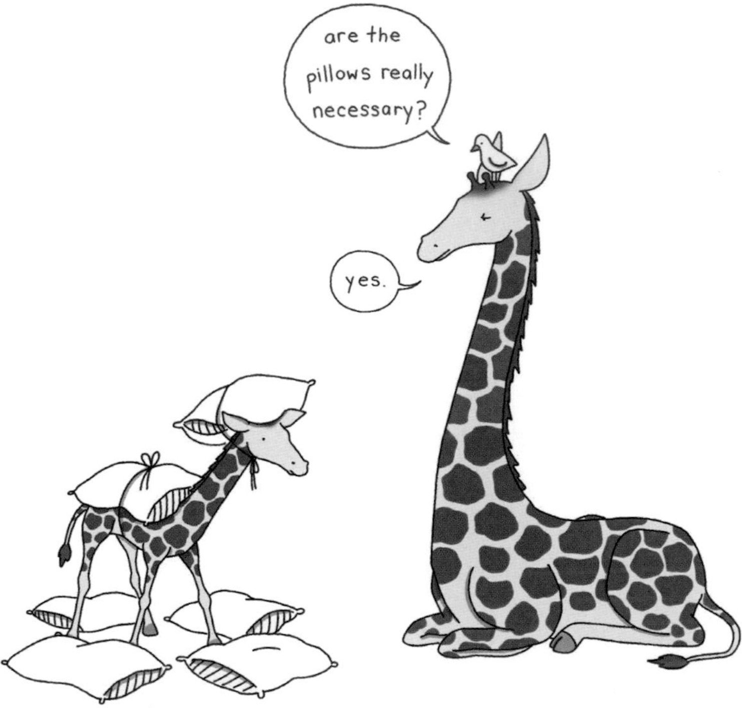
are the pillows really necessary?
yes.

Sometimes, you connect immediately.

Sometimes, you don't.

(Which is perfectly normal, by the way.)

These early weeks can be challenging. Luckily, everyone has plenty of advice for you.

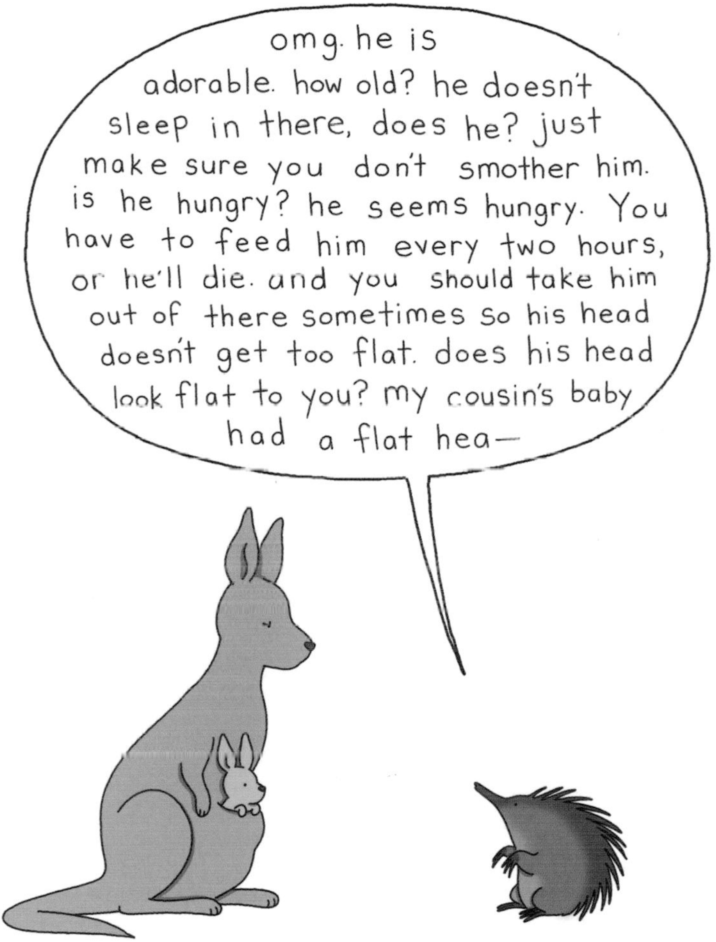
omg. he is adorable. how old? he doesn't sleep in there, does he? just make sure you don't smother him. is he hungry? he seems hungry. You have to feed him every two hours, or he'll die. and you should take him out of there sometimes so his head doesn't get too flat. does his head look flat to you? my cousin's baby had a flat hea—

Remember sleep?

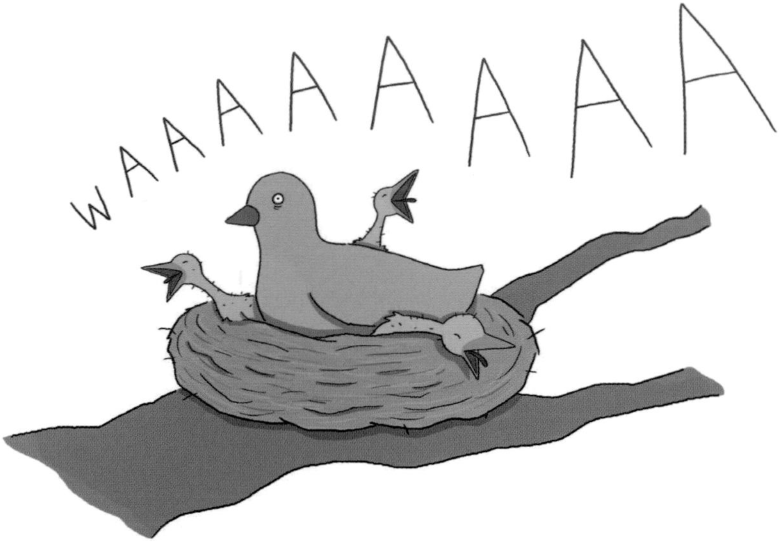
WAAAAAAAA

Well, you won't.

There will also be mood swings . . .

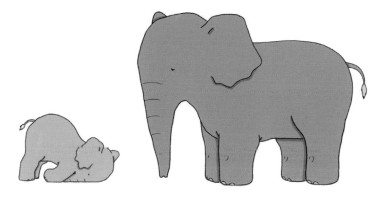

. . . and not much
time to yourself.

You may not recognize
yourself for a while.

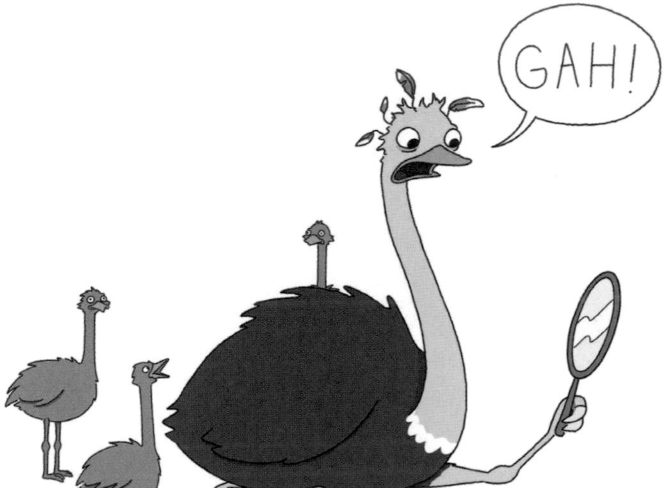
GAH!

Sometimes, you may even feel
you've lost a little bit of yourself.

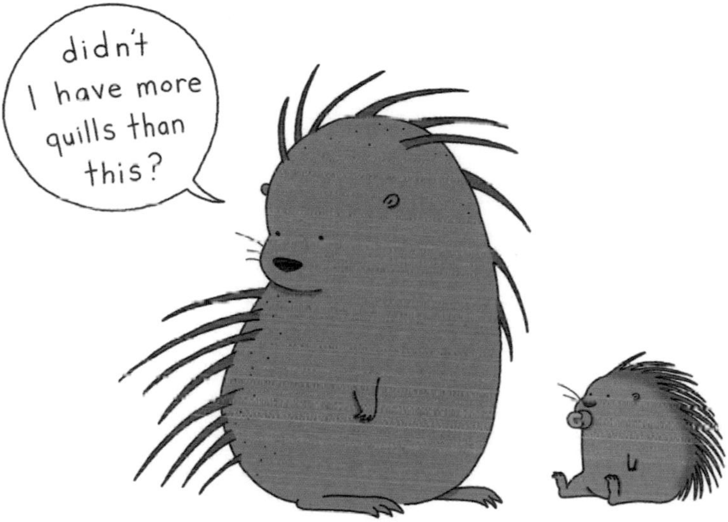
didn't I have more quills than this?

This part may feel like
it will last forever, but it
won't.

Days
Without
Sleep
卌 卌 卌
卌 卌 卌
卌 卌 卌
|||

One day, the infant phase will end . . .

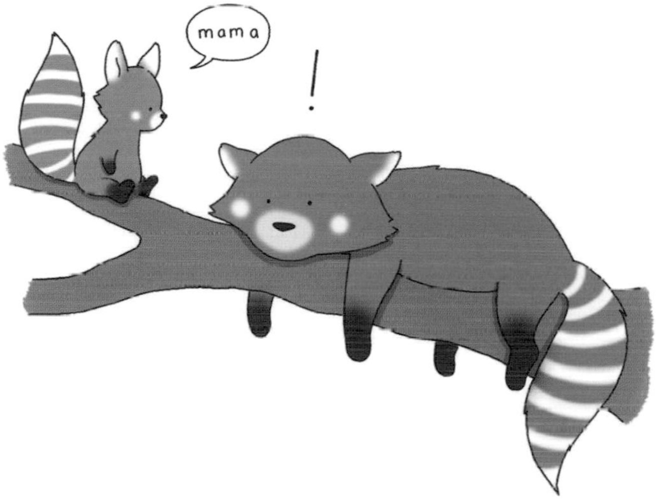
mam a
!

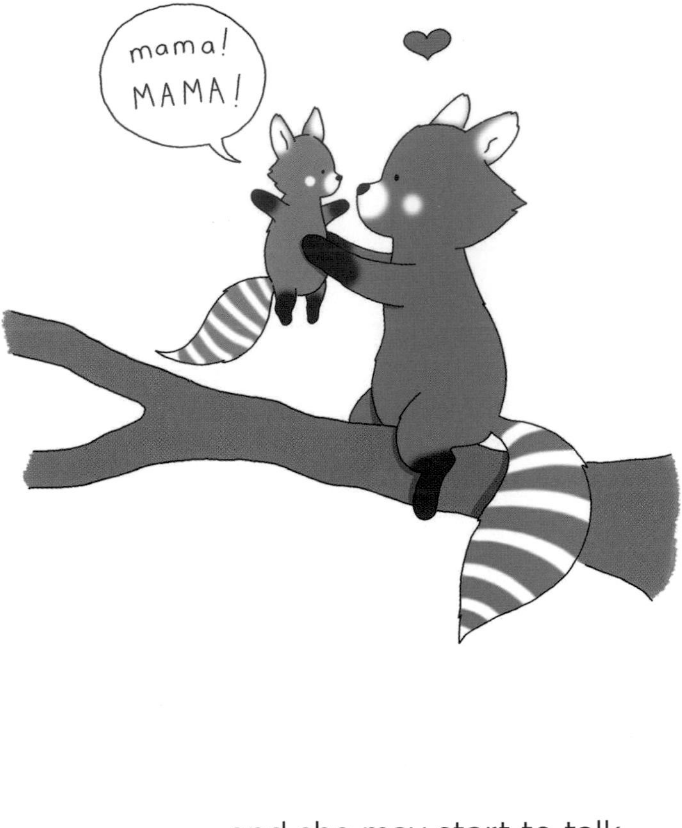
mama!
MAMA!

. . . and she may start to talk . . .

. . . and she may never . . .

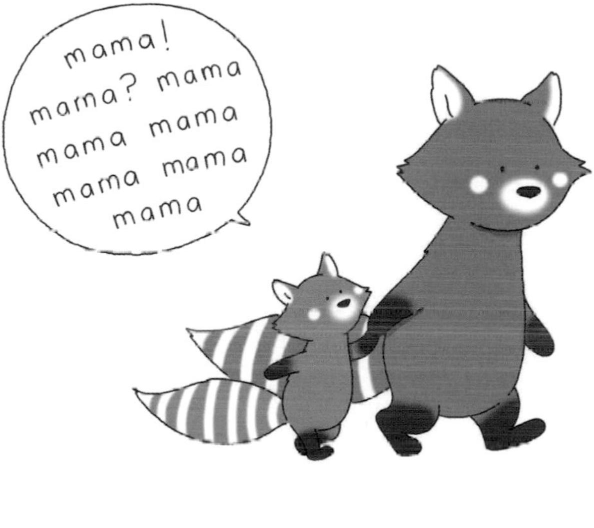
mama!
mama? mama
mama mama
mama mama
mama

. . . ever . . .

. . . stop.

Remember when you
thought having a newborn
was hard?

Wait until you have a toddler.

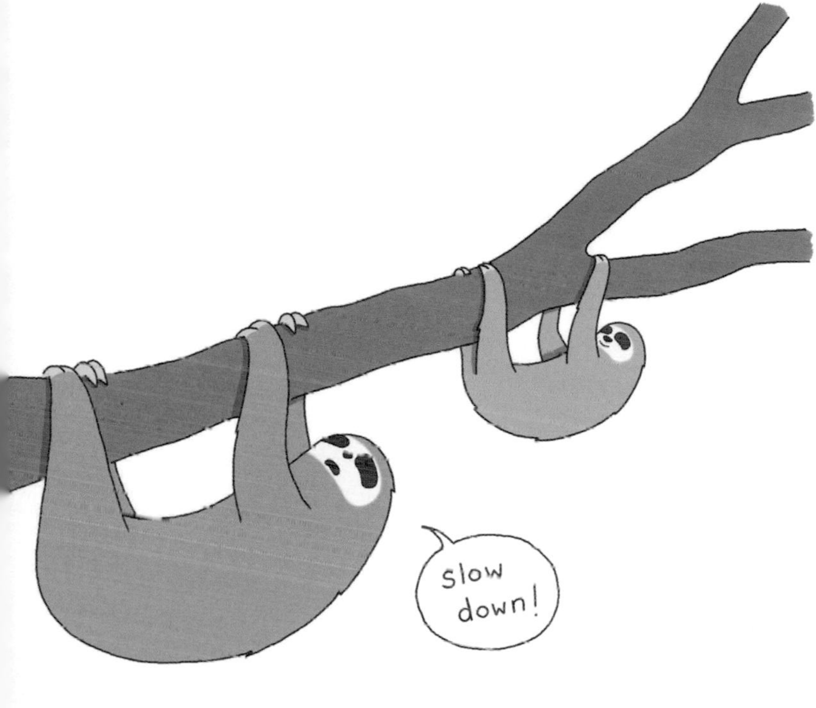
slow down!

There will be a lot of questions.

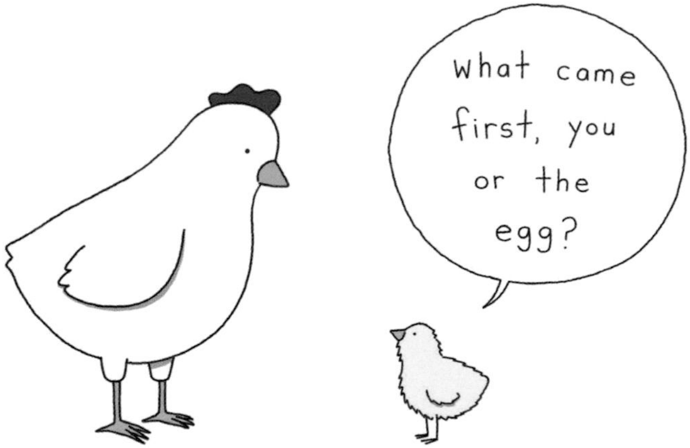
What came first, you or the egg?

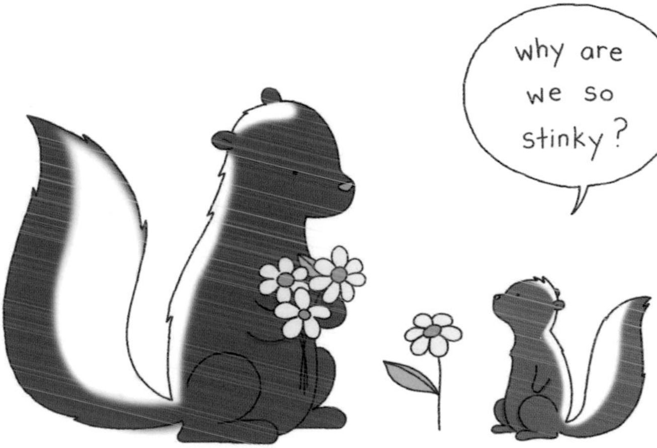
why are we so stinky?

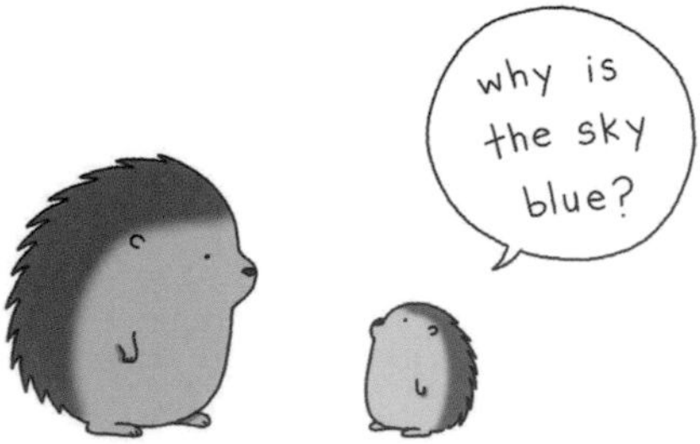
why is the sky blue?

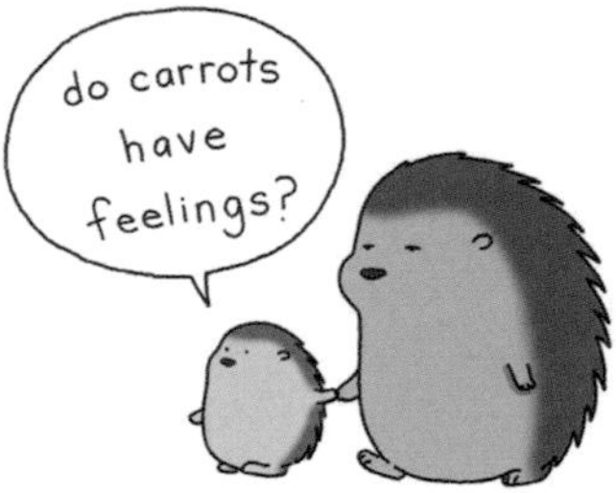
do carrots have feelings?

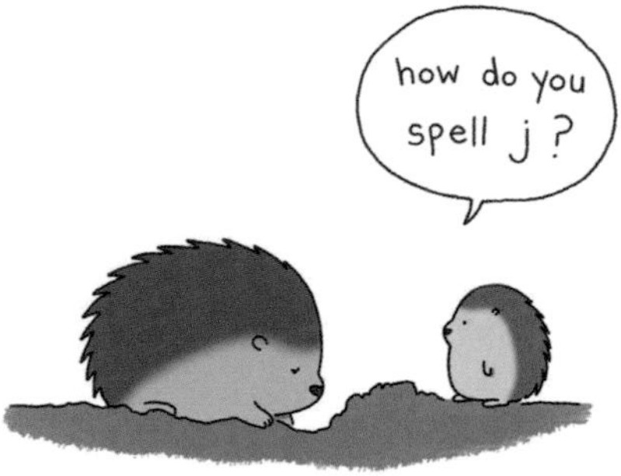
how do you spell j ?

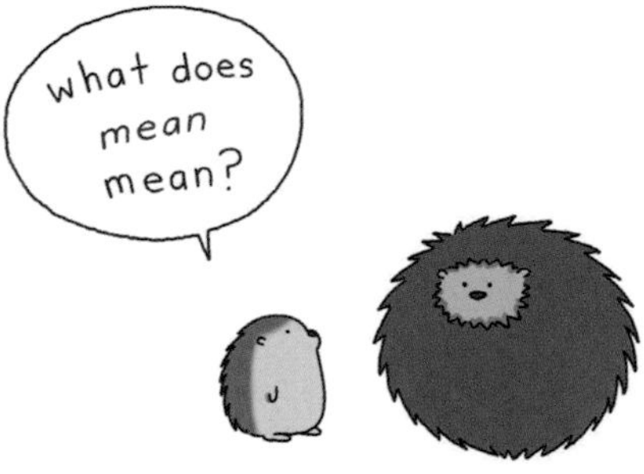
what does mean mean?

Seriously, a LOT.

And there will be plenty of fun.

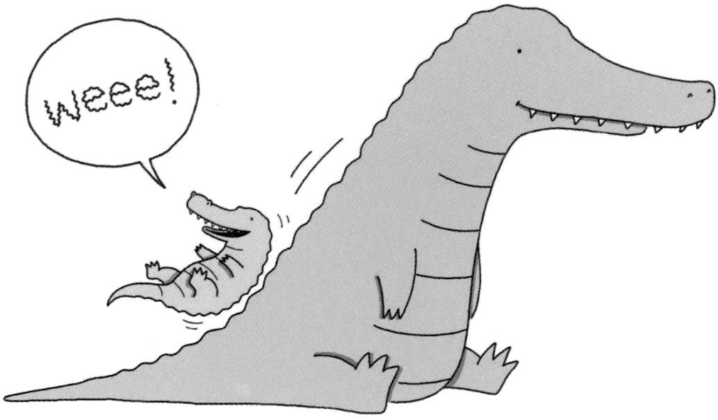
weee!

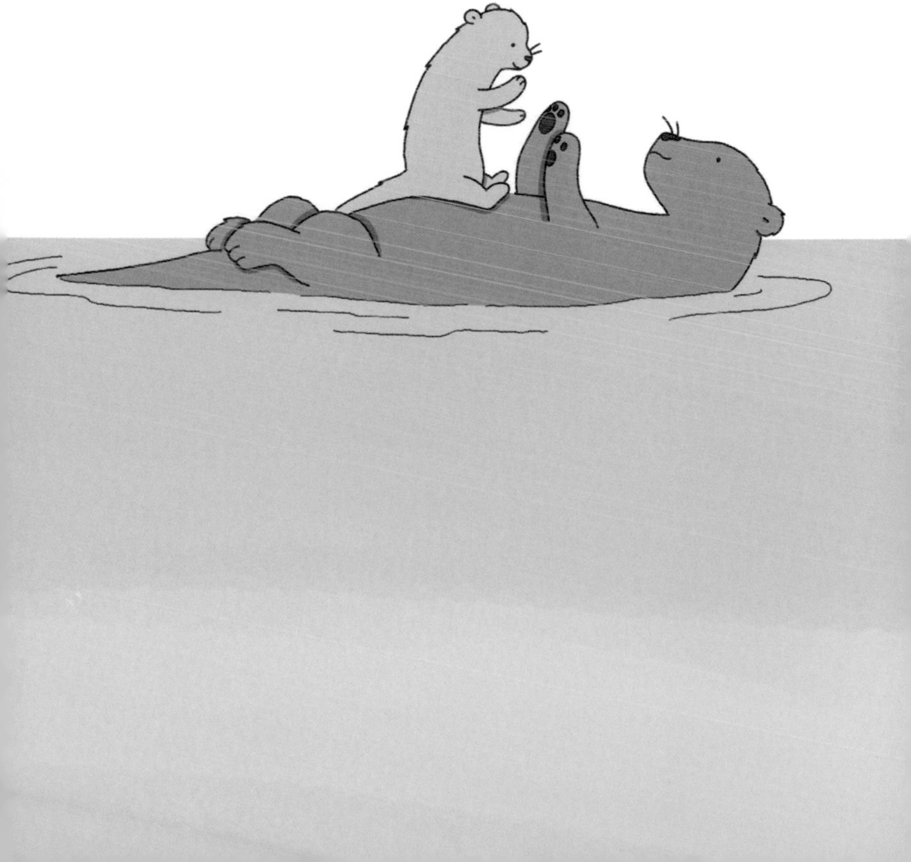

Before you know it,
your baby will be a kid . . .

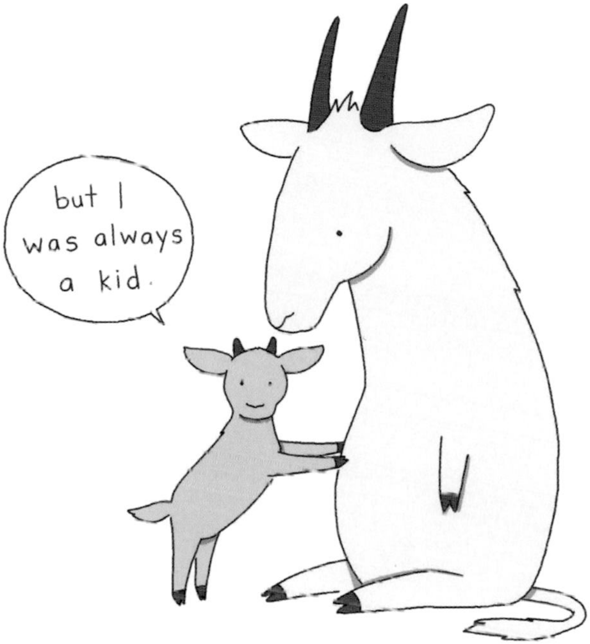
but I was always a kid.

(You know what I mean.)

. . . and he may start to
become more independent.

There will be some embarrassing moments.

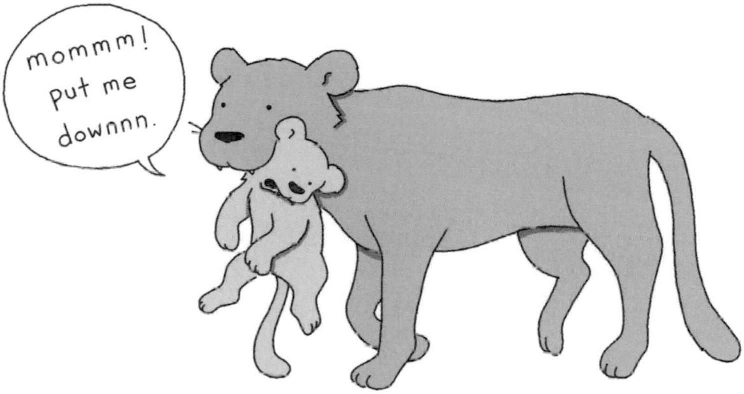
mommm! put me downnn.

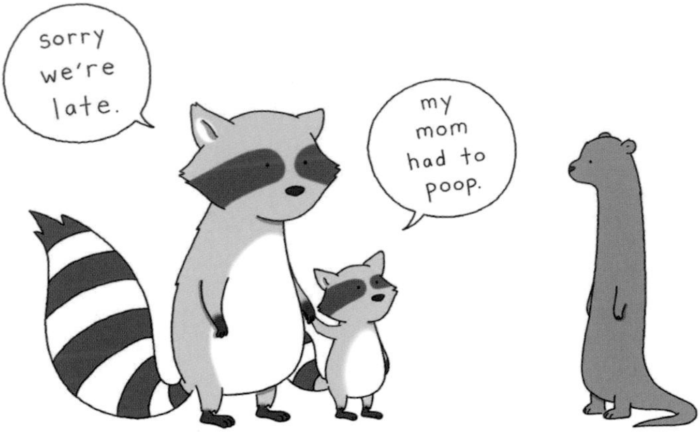
sorry we're late.
my mom had to poop.

(For both of you.)

There will also be learning moments.

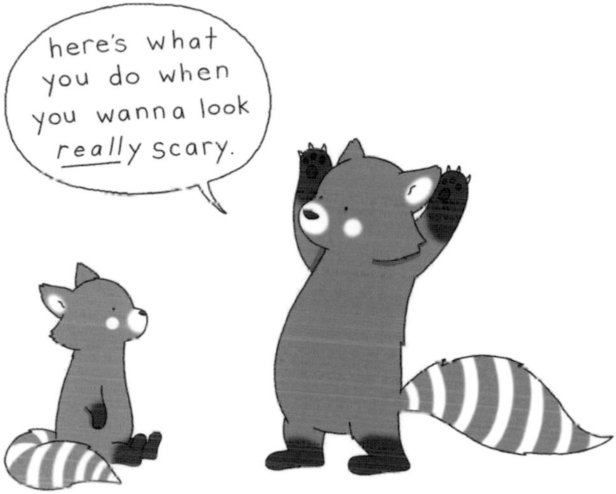
here's what you do when you wanna look really scary.

(For both of you.)

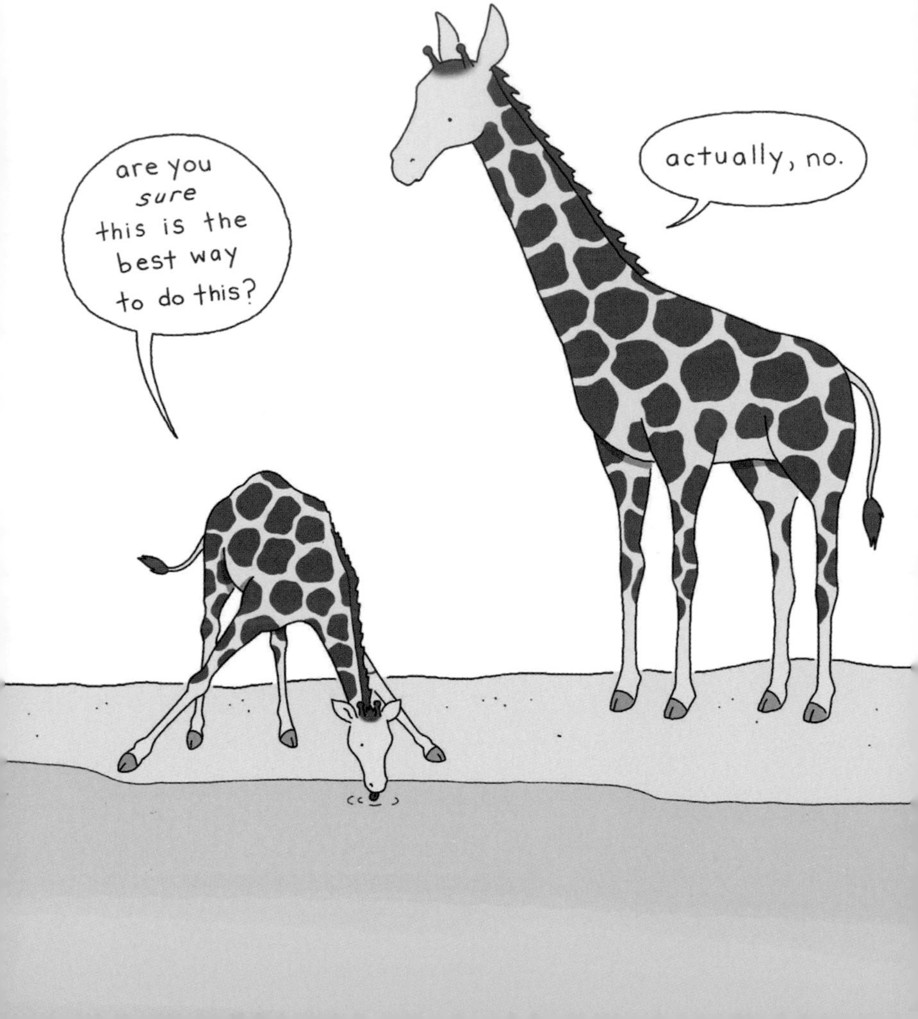
are you *sure* this is the best way to do this?
actually, no.

Soon, you'll have a teenager.

THEY'RE FUN!

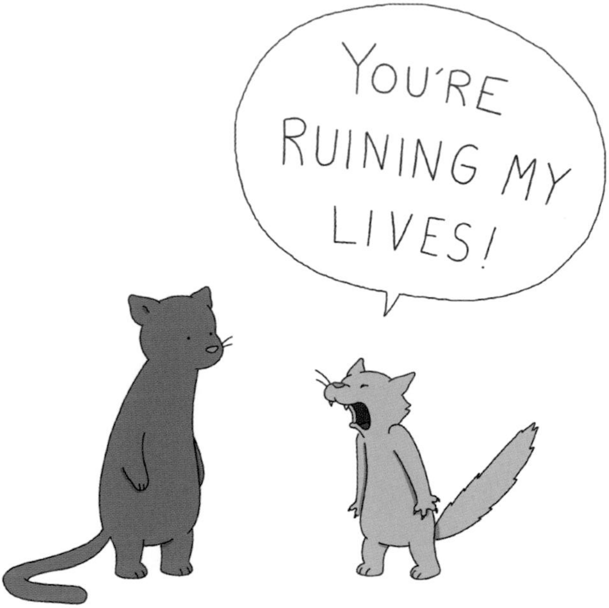
YOU'RE RUINING MY LIVES!

There will be disagreements . . .

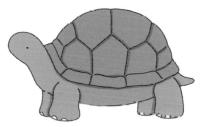

I HATE
YOU!

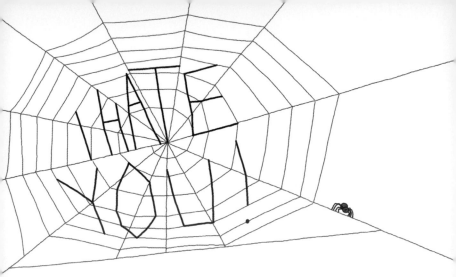

. . . and plenty of drama.

But there will
also be late-night
conversations . . .

. . . and laughter . . .

. . . and lots . . .

. . . and lots . . .

LOVE
YOU!

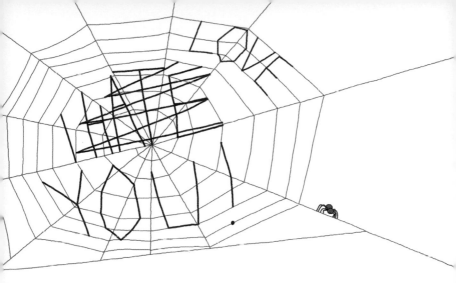

. . . of love.

Where has the time gone?

It seems like only a month ago,
he was a chick.

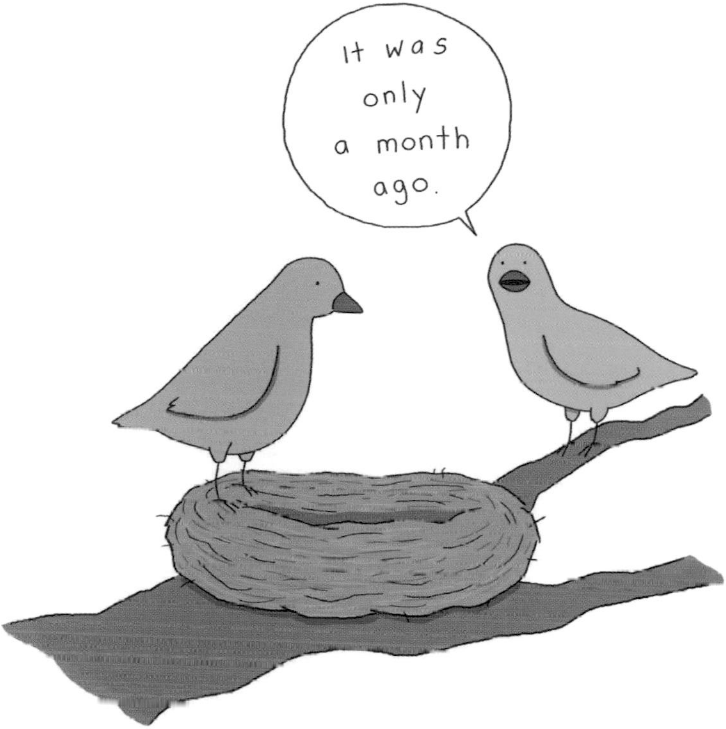
It was only a month ago.

(You know what I mean.)

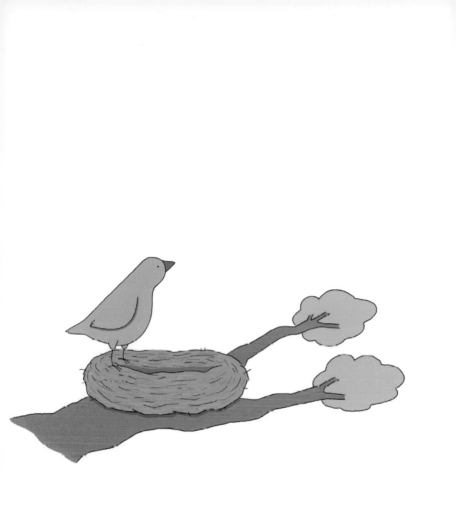

This part is hard.

But you aren't alone!

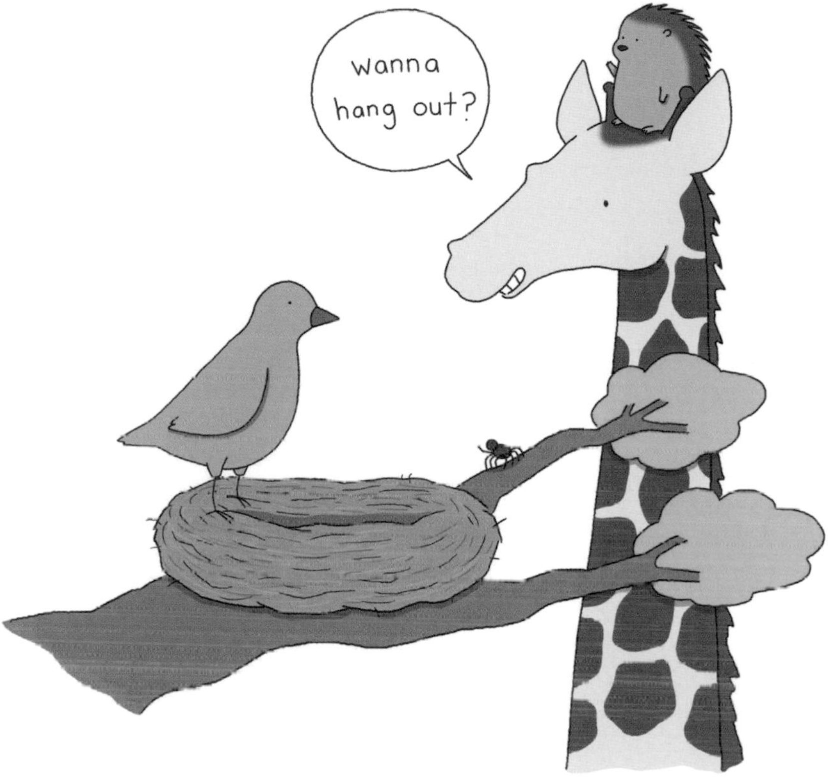
wanna hang out?

And you can handle it.

After all, moms have been doing
this for millions of years.

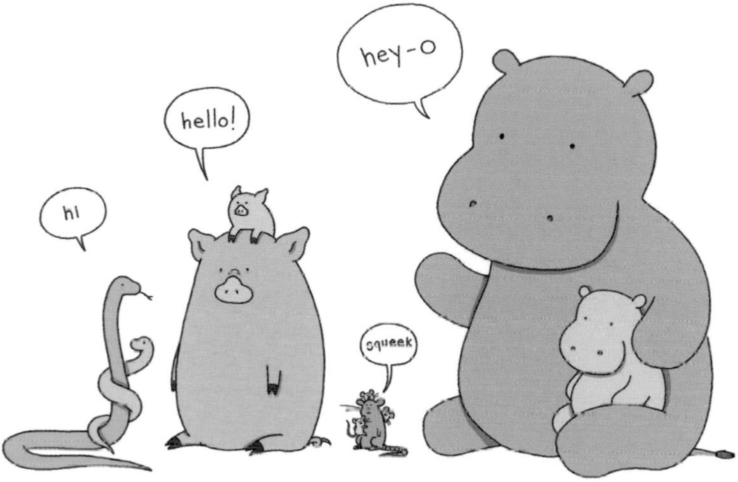
hi
hello!
squeek
hey-o

And there are billions of other moms
out there, in all shapes and sizes.

There are younger moms.

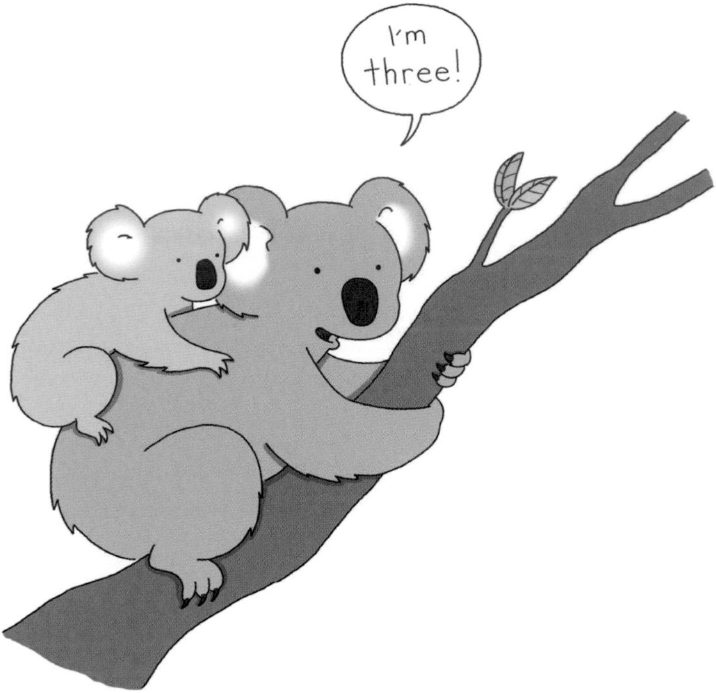
I'm three!

And older moms.

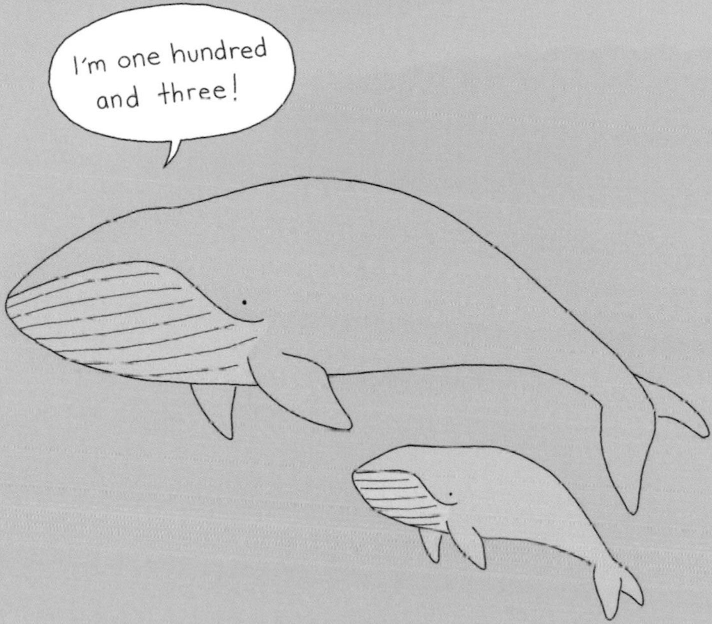
I'm one hundred and three!

Moms who look like their kids.

And moms who don't.

There are grandparents who are moms.

Cousins, sisters, and
friends who are moms.

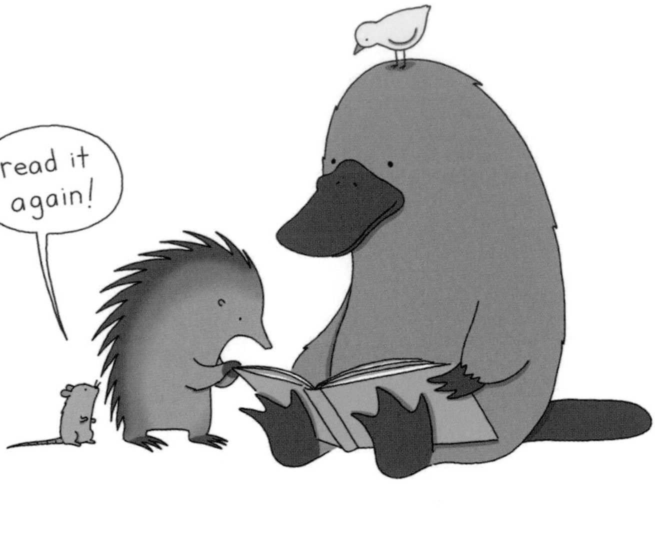
read it again!

Stepmoms and foster moms.

Moms who have yearned.

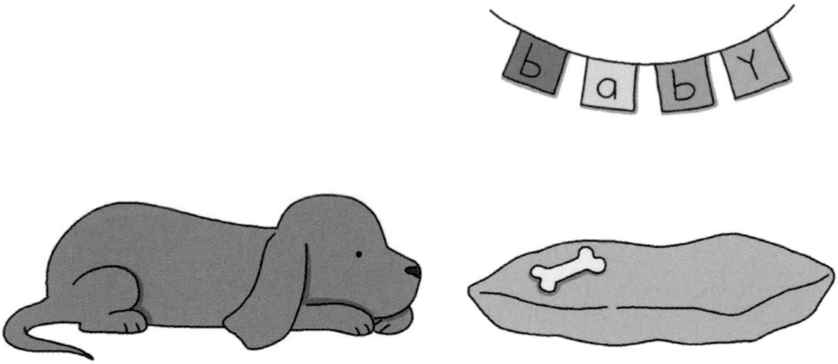
b a b Y

And moms who have lost.

Some families have more than one mom.

Or a parent who takes on the role of mom.

There are moms
who go to work.

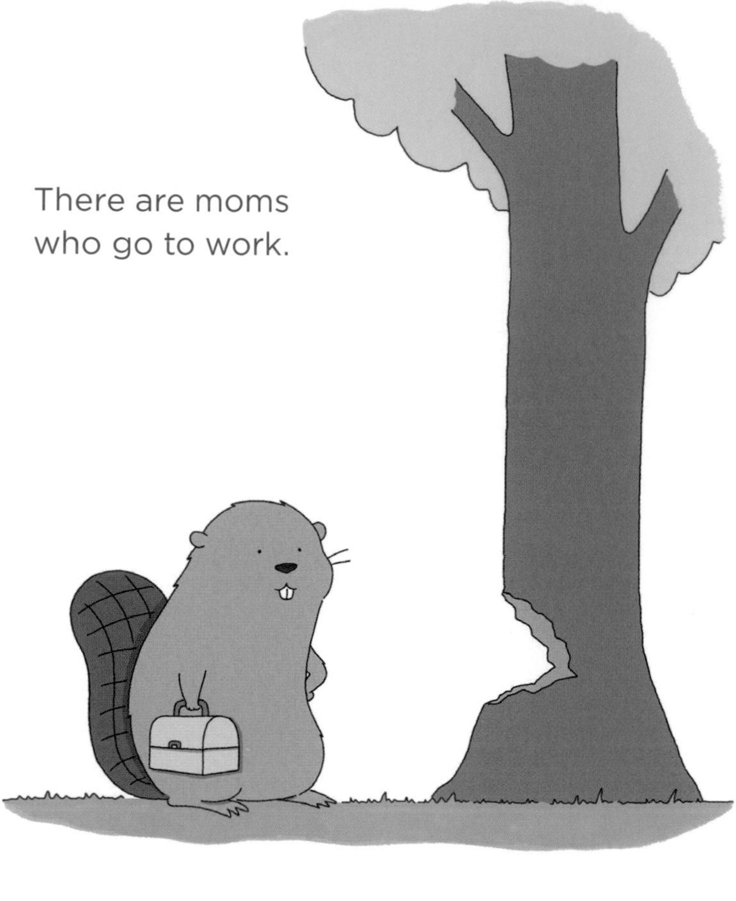

And moms who stay home.

(They're working, too!)

Moms who have help.

thanks!
I'll be home
around 5.

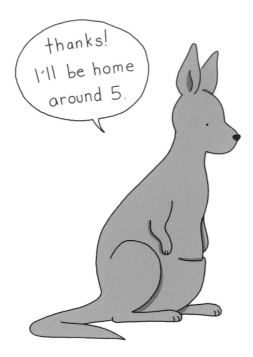

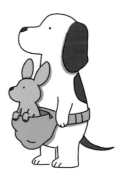

Moms who do it alone.

Moms who never leave their kids alone.

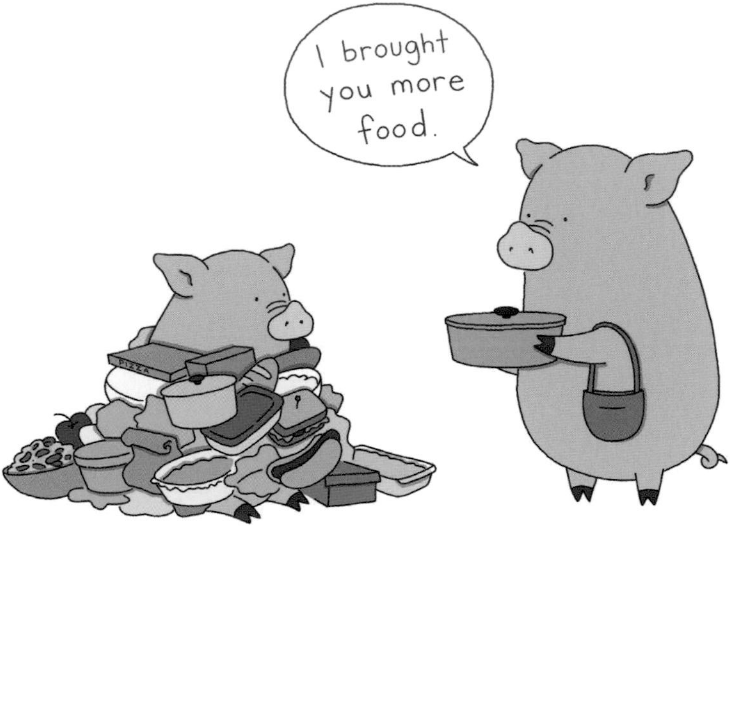
I brought you more food.
PIZZA

Moms who leave much too soon.

This part is hard.

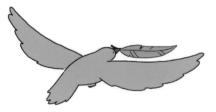

But moms never *really* leave.

Because your words . . .

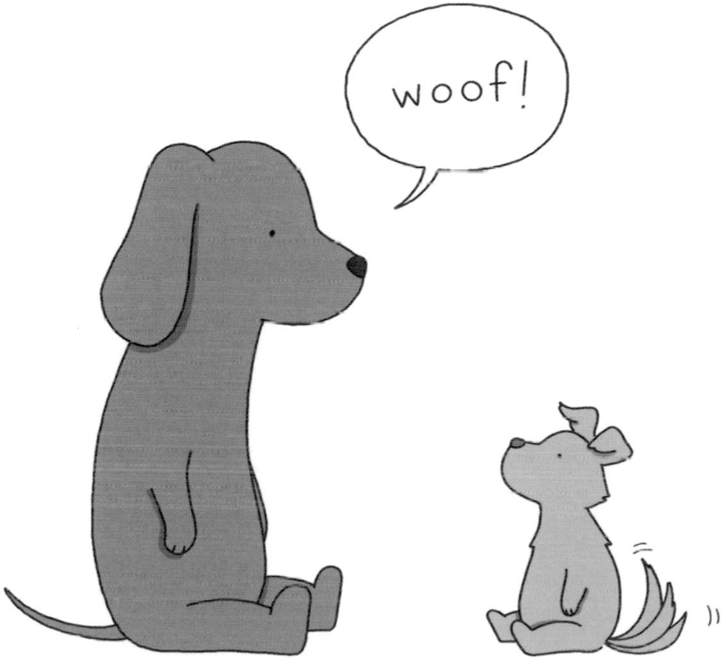
woof!

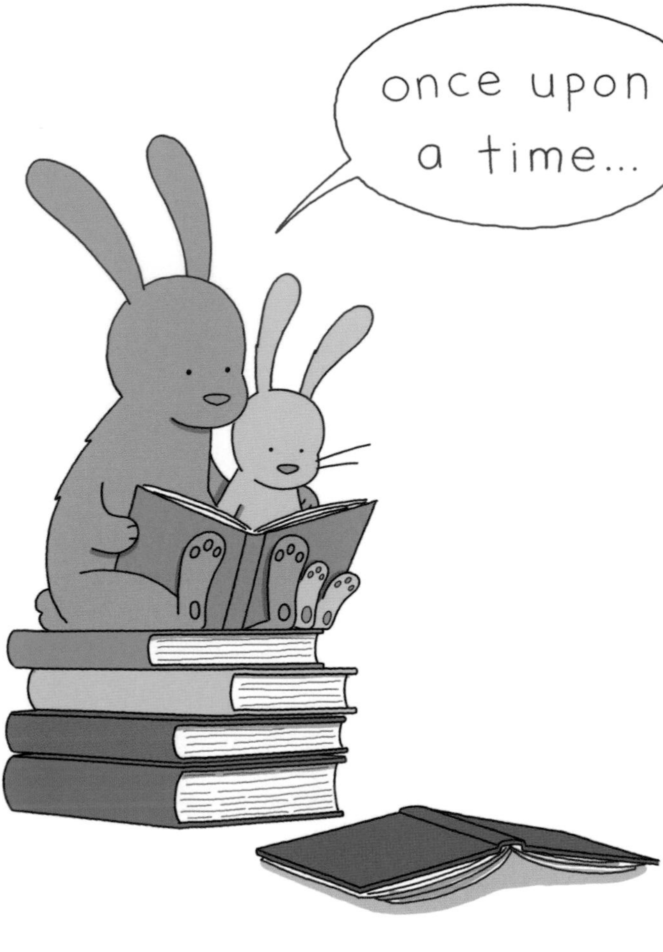
once upon
a time...

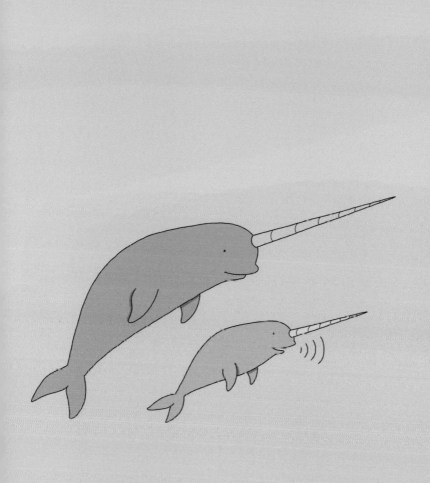

. . . become her words.

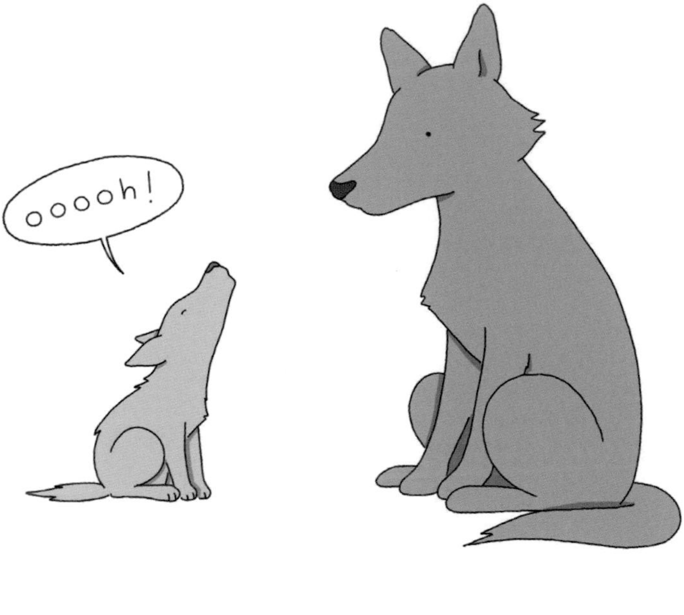
ooooh!

Your lessons . . .

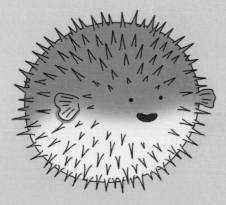

. . . become his lessons.

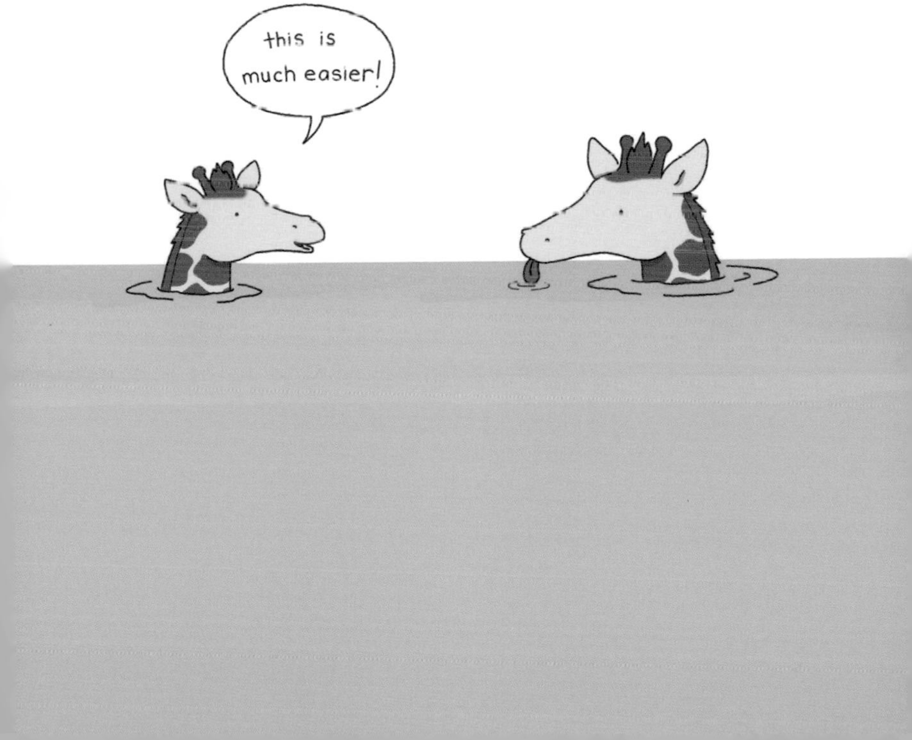
this is
much easier!

do I look scary?
extremely.

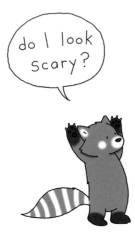

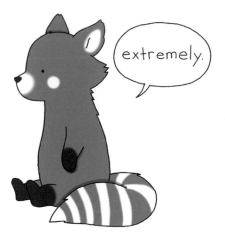

Your love . . .

. . . becomes her love.

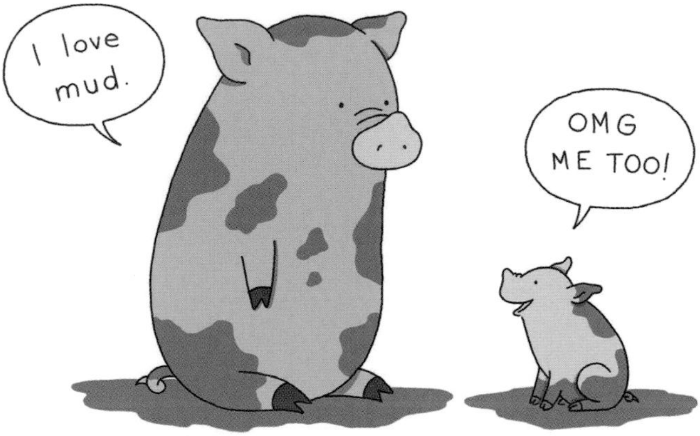
I love mud.
OMG ME TOO!

Because there is no
love as powerful . . .

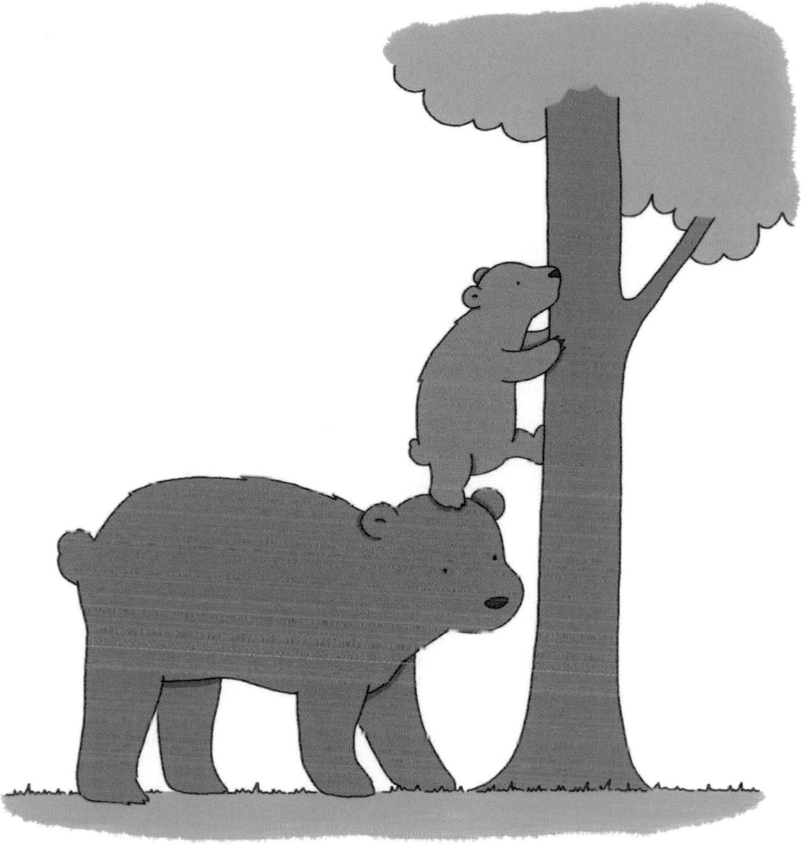

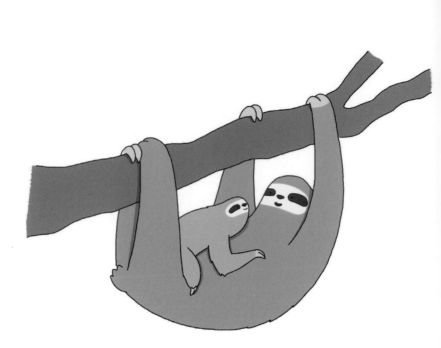

. . . as a mother's love.

And that never goes away.

But seriously, if you have a baby
joining your house soon, get some
sleep now—like, RIGHT now. While
you still can!

Trust me, you'll need your rest.

Because you're mom.

And there is no job on earth . . .

. . . more important than yours.

# Acknowledgments

I would like to say thanks to whoever is holding this book right now. Whether you've seen my work before or are looking at it now for the first time, thank you so much for your support. To Kathleen Ortiz, and everyone at New Leaf Literary, for their continuous hard work. Sarah Murphy, and everyone at Flatiron Books, for believing in this project and helping me realize the vision for it. To my family and friends, who helped give me feedback on this book in its early stages, and who helped inspire much of its content. My brother, sister, and dad, for their constant and continuous support. My husband, who I am so lucky to have as both a partner and friend, and who is always willing to give honest, creative feedback. To my mom, who taught me what unconditional love is, and my daughter, who reminds me what it is every day.

# About the Author

**LIZ CLIMO** grew up in the San Francisco Bay Area and moved to Los Angeles after college to work as a character artist on *The Simpsons*. She started the popular Instagram comic series *The Little World of Liz Climo* at @lizclimo, which became her debut comic collection. She is also the author and illustrator of several comics and children's books. Liz currently lives in Los Angeles with her husband and their daughter.